ACHIEVE LEVEL 3

Maths

BY RICHARD COOPER AND SHIRLEY ARMER

ADDITIONAL MATERIAL BY JANE BOVEY

RISING STARS

Rising Stars UK Ltd., 76 Farnaby Road, Bromley, BR1 4BH
Website: www.risingstars-uk.com

Every effort has been made to trace copyright holders and obtain
their permission for the use of copyright material. The authors
and publishers will gladly receive information enabling them to
rectify any error or omission in subsequent editions.

All facts are correct at time of going to press.

New Edition 2003
Published 2003
First published 2002
Text, design and layout © Rising Stars UK Ltd.

Editorial: Tanya Solomons
Design: Starfish Design for Print
Illustrations: copyright © Burville-Riley
Cover photo: copyright © Getty Images

British Library Cataloguing in Publication Data
A CIP record for this book is available from the British Library.

ISBN 1-904591-30-2

Printed at Wyndham Gait, Grimsby, UK

Contents

How to use this book

Each topic is covered in a similar way:

1 **Introduction section** – This section tells you what your child needs to do to get a Level 3. It picks out what the key learning objective is and explains it simply.

2 **The question** – The question helps your child to 'learn by doing'. It is presented in a similar way to the SATs questions and gives you a real example to work with.

3 **The flow chart** – This shows the steps to use when completing questions. Some of the advice happens on every flow chart (Read the question then read it again).

4 **The Star Tips** – How to get to grips with each topic.

5 **The Star characters** – Maths Star is the character who takes the children through the book. He explains the concepts being covered and offers support and an encouraging word at the right time.

6 **Practice questions** – This is where the children have to do the work! Try each question using the technique explained in the flow chart and then check the answers at the back.

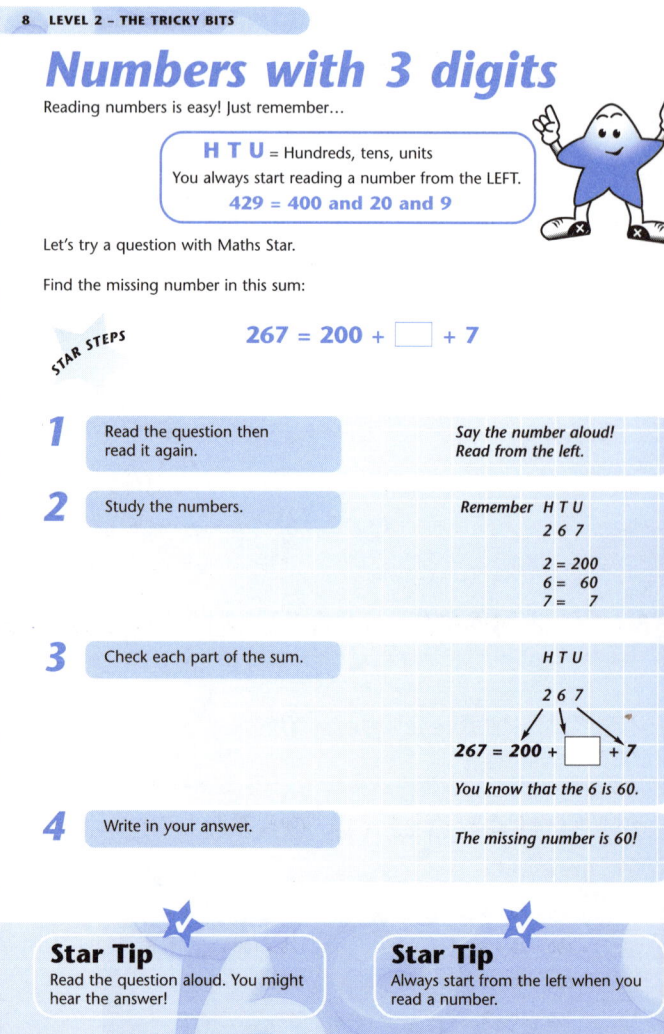

8 LEVEL 2 – THE TRICKY BITS

Numbers with 3 digits

Reading numbers is easy! Just remember…

H T U = Hundreds, tens, units
You always start reading a number from the LEFT.
429 = 400 and 20 and 9

Let's try a question with Maths Star.

Find the missing number in this sum:

STAR STEPS

267 = 200 + ☐ + 7

1 Read the question then read it again.   Say the number aloud! Read from the left.

2 Study the numbers.   Remember H T U
                                              2 6 7

                                              2 = 200
                                              6 = 60
                                              7 =   7

3 Check each part of the sum.   H T U
                                  2 6 7

                                  267 = 200 + ☐ + 7
                                  You know that the 6 is 60.

4 Write in your answer.   The missing number is 60!

Star Tip
Read the question aloud. You might hear the answer!

Star Tip
Always start from the left when you read a number.

LEVEL 2 – THE TRICKY BITS   9

ou can be a Maths superstar! Try another question.

ut a number in the box below to make the sum correct.

STEPS

[ ] + 50 + 2 = 352

1 Read the question then read it again.

Say the number aloud!
Read from the left.

2 Study the numbers.

Remember H T U
3 5 2
3 = 300
5 = 50
2 = 2

3 Check each part of the sum.

H T U

352

[ ] + 50 + 2 = 352

You know that the 3 is 300.

4 Write in your answer.

The missing number is 300!

Practice questions

Practise reading and writing hundreds, tens and units.	Practise finding the missing number.
300 + 20 + 1 = [ ]	200 + 40 + [ ] = 249
700 + 50 + 9 = [ ]	800 + [ ] + 5 = 835
200 + 70 + 3 = [ ]	[ ] + 90 + 2 = 492
900 + 10 + 4 = [ ]	700 + [ ] + 4 = 724

Now try some this way!	Try them this way too!
[ ] = 400 + 70 + 5	523 = [ ] + 20 + 3
[ ] = 100 + 30 + 2	178 = 100 + [ ] + 8
[ ] = 600 + 40 + 7	356 = 300 + [ ] + 6
[ ] = 500 + 10 + 9	649 = [ ] + 40 + 9

How to use the book with your child:

1 Focus on ONE topic each time. Read through the introduction and the question.

2 Follow the flow chart through (make notes if it helps your child).

3 Try some practice questions.

4 Check your answers and look again at the Star Tips and flow chart.

What we have included:

We have put in those topics at Level 1 and 2 that children often find difficult. These are at the front of the book and give a more gentle introduction to the material. They are presented in a similar way to the Level 3 content, so doing this section first will help children to become accustomed to the style of the books.

We have also included all the answers to the practice questions!

GOOD LUCK!

Number bonds to 5

It's really important to get these number bonds into your head. They can be just as useful as knowing ALL your tables and they can help you to learn your tables too!

1 0 + ☐ = 5

2 1 + ☐ = 5

3 2 + ☐ = 5

4 3 + ☐ = 5

5 4 + ☐ = 5

6 5 + ☐ = 5

7 ☐ + 0 = 5

8 ☐ + 1 = 5

9 ☐ + 2 = 5

10 ☐ + 3 = 5

11 ☐ + 4 = 5

12 ☐ + 5 = 5

Of course, once you have mastered the addition then subtraction shouldn't be too hard. Have a go at these questions.

1 5 − ☐ = 0

2 5 − ☐ = 1

3 5 − ☐ = 2

4 5 − ☐ = 3

5 5 − ☐ = 4

6 5 − ☐ = 5

7 ☐ − 0 = 5

8 ☐ − 1 = 4

9 ☐ − 2 = 3

10 ☐ − 3 = 2

11 ☐ − 4 = 1

12 ☐ − 5 = 0

Star Tip

Remember that if all else fails, you can use your fingers.

Five fingers game

Show some fingers from one hand to a friend. Your friend has to say how many more make 5! Take turns to test each other. The more you practise, the better you'll get!

Number bonds to 10

Learning these number bonds is a bit difficult because the numbers are bigger and there are more of them. But if you can learn them, they will really help your mental maths!

1 $0 + \boxed{} = 10$

2 $1 + \boxed{} = 10$

3 $2 + \boxed{} = 10$

4 $3 + \boxed{} = 10$

5 $4 + \boxed{} = 10$

6 $5 + \boxed{} = 10$

7 $6 + \boxed{} = 10$

8 $7 + \boxed{} = 10$

9 $8 + \boxed{} = 10$

10 $9 + \boxed{} = 10$

11 $10 + \boxed{} = 10$

12 $\boxed{} + 0 = 10$

13 $\boxed{} + 1 = 10$

14 $\boxed{} + 2 = 10$

15 $\boxed{} + 3 = 10$

16 $\boxed{} + 4 = 10$

17 $\boxed{} + 5 = 10$

18 $\boxed{} + 6 = 10$

19 $\boxed{} + 7 = 10$

20 $\boxed{} + 8 = 10$

21 $\boxed{} + 9 = 10$

22 $\boxed{} + 10 = 10$

Now have a go with subtraction to 10. If you can get these, you'll be a superstar!

1 $\boxed{} - 0 = 10$

2 $\boxed{} - 1 = 10$

3 $\boxed{} - 2 = 10$

4 $\boxed{} - 3 = 10$

5 $\boxed{} - 4 = 10$

6 $\boxed{} - 5 = 10$

7 $\boxed{} - 6 = 10$

8 $\boxed{} - 7 = 10$

9 $\boxed{} - 8 = 10$

10 $\boxed{} - 9 = 10$

11 $\boxed{} - 10 = 10$

Now try these.

12 $8 - 7 = \boxed{}$

13 $7 - 2 = \boxed{}$

14 $9 - 6 = \boxed{}$

15 $3 - 2 = \boxed{}$

16 $5 - 1 = \boxed{}$

17 $1 - 1 = \boxed{}$

18 $2 - 1 = \boxed{}$

19 $5 - 0 = \boxed{}$

20 $6 - 3 = \boxed{}$

21 $9 - 4 = \boxed{}$

22 $9 - 1 = \boxed{}$

Star Tip
You can use these sums to help you with numbers up to 100. Just add a 0 to each number.

Numbers with 3 digits

Reading numbers is easy! Just remember…

> **H T U** = Hundreds, tens, units
> You always start reading a number from the LEFT.
> **429 = 400 and 20 and 9**

Let's try a question with Maths Star.

Find the missing number in this sum:

$$267 = 200 + \boxed{} + 7$$

1 | Read the question then read it again. | *Say the number aloud! Read from the left.*

2 | Study the numbers. | *Remember* H T U
       | | 2 6 7

$2 = 200$
$6 = 60$
$7 = 7$

3 | Check each part of the sum. | H T U

2 6 7

$$267 = 200 + \boxed{} + 7$$

You know that the 6 is 60.

4 | Write in your answer. | *The missing number is 60!*

Star Tip
Read the question aloud. You might hear the answer!

Star Tip
Always start from the left when you read a number.

You can be a Maths superstar! Try another question.

Put a number in the box below to make the sum correct.

$$\boxed{} + 50 + 2 = 352$$

STAR STEPS

1 Read the question then read it again.

Say the number aloud! Read from the left.

2 Study the numbers.

Remember H T U
3 5 2
3 = 300
5 = 50
2 = 2

3 Check each part of the sum.

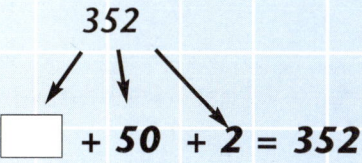

H T U

352

$$\boxed{} + 50 + 2 = 352$$

You know that the 3 is 300.

4 Write in your answer.

The missing number is 300!

Practice questions

Practise reading and writing hundreds, tens and units.

300 + 20 + 1 = ☐

700 + 50 + 9 = ☐

200 + 70 + 3 = ☐

900 + 10 + 4 = ☐

Now try some this way!

☐ = 400 + 70 + 5

☐ = 100 + 30 + 2

☐ = 600 + 40 + 7

☐ = 500 + 10 + 9

Practise finding the missing number.

200 + 40 + ☐ = 249

800 + ☐ + 5 = 835

☐ + 90 + 2 = 492

700 + ☐ + 4 = 724

Try them this way too!

523 = ☐ + 20 + 3

178 = 100 + ☐ + 8

356 = 300 + ☐ + 6

649 = ☐ + 40 + 9

Checking your answers

Do you remember that addition and subtraction are opposites? This means that they are INVERSE. You can check addition sums using subtraction and you can check subtraction sums using addition! Amazing!

Watch: 8 + 2 = 10   10 − 2 = 8 and 10 − 8 = 2
We can use this to see if we have got our answers right.

STAR STEPS

Question: 24 + 4 = ☐

1 Read the question then read it again.

OK, we have to find the answer to an addition sum.

2 Do your sum.

24 + 4 = 26

3 First, does your answer look right?

Uh-oh! No, in the units column 4 + 4 = 6!

4 If not, you can check using the INVERSE.

Right, inverse means OPPOSITE. The opposite of addition is subtraction, so I will use subtraction to check.

26 − 24 = 2

5 The answer is wrong, it should be 24.
If your check sum does not fit your first sum then re-do your first sum.

OK, let's get it right this time.

24 + 4 = 28

Now check again!

Answer these sums and then check the answers using the INVERSE.

1 12 − 7 = ☐   **4** 28 − 13 = ☐

2 15 + 11 = ☐   **5** 37 + 24 = ☐

3 29 + 22 = ☐   **6** 43 − 18 = ☐

Star Tip

With INVERSE, addition can be done in ANY order but subtraction will give you different answers if you change the order. Try it and see.

Solving multi-step problems

You may be asked a question like this:

STAR STEPS

> **Mary has 12 balloons. Three of them pop and two blow away. Her friend Jeff gives Mary 8 of his balloons. How many balloons does Mary have now?**

1 | Read the question then read it again. | *There are lots of words. Read slowly and carefully.*

2 | Which numbers are given in the question? | *OK, 12, 3, 2 and 8. What should I do with them?*

3 | Now decide which operations (+, −, x, ÷) you need to do. | *"three pop" = subtract*
"two are blown away" = subtract
"gives her 8 of his" = addition

4 | Do the sum step by step. | *12 − 3 = 9*
9 − 2 = 7
7 + 8 = 15

5 | Check your answer. | *That's right.*
Mary has 15 balloons.

Practice question

> **Sara has 6 sweets. Daniel has 7 sweets. Trevor has 8 more sweets than Sara and Daniel together. How many sweets does Trevor have?**

Star Tip

Don't rush these questions. Think clearly and take your time.

Interpreting written instructions

Reading Star, Writing Star, oh… and I, always agree on one thing.

★ **Read the question… then… read it again!**

This will help you work out what you have to do to get the right answer.

This is a type of question you will be asked a lot.

Ann measured the height of these 2 dolls in blocks. How many blocks taller is the large doll?

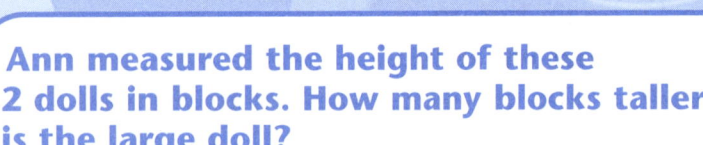 **blocks**

Can you explain how you worked out your answer?

Which word in the question is key to answering this question? Draw a ring around it.

Here are two more questions:

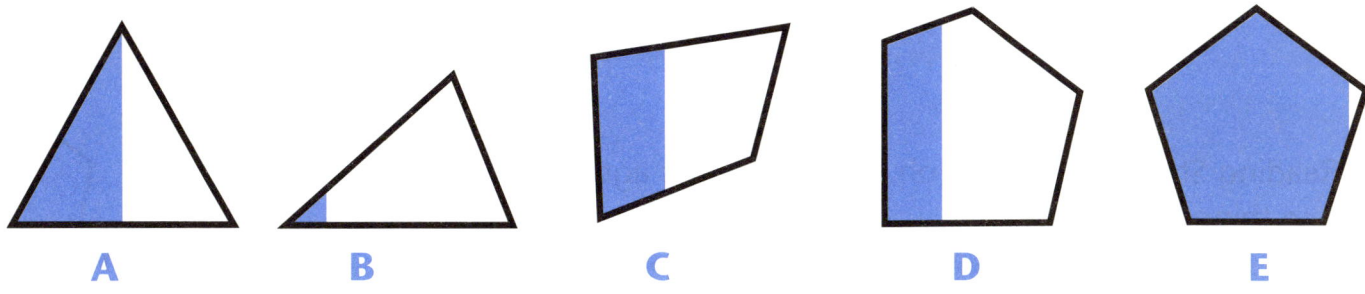

1 Write the letter of the shape that is more than half blue here.   A

Tom got this question wrong because he didn't read the words 'more than'.

Remember to read the question, then read it again before moving on. You can circle or underline words that will help you to answer the question as you go along.

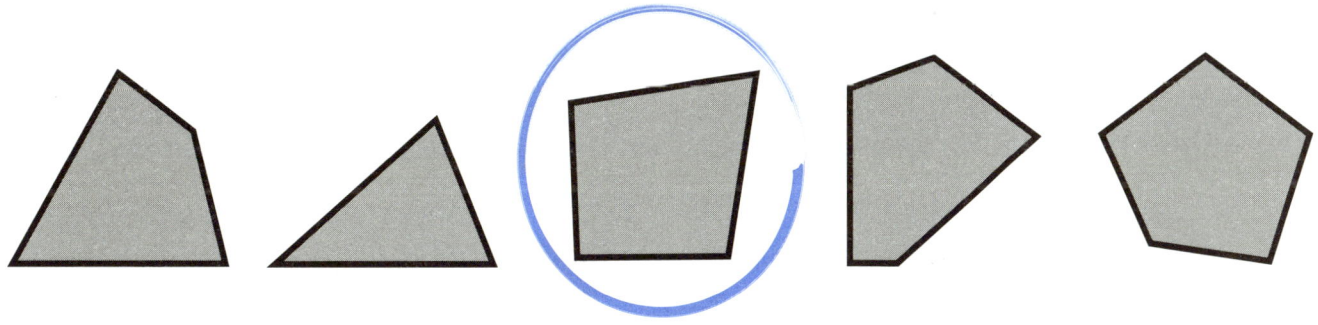

2 Circle two shapes that have four sides.

Joanne got this question wrong. She didn't circle two shapes with four sides, just one.

Remember to read the question and check your answer at the end. You can check your answer by reading the question again and then looking at your answer.

Star Tip

If you don't want to make any mistakes:

★ Read the question.
★ Read it again!
★ Think about the words and numbers you have read.

Place value up to 1000

Each number is made up from digits. Where these digits are in a number gives that number its value.

	Hundreds	Tens	Units	
784	7	8	4	= 700 + 80 + 4

Question: Write in the missing number.

STAR STEPS

	Hundreds	Tens	Units	
	3	5	9	= 300 + ☐ + 9

1 Read the question then read it again. → *What number am I going to write in the box?*

2 Which column is the number missing from? → *The middle one – that's the tens column.*

3 Which digit is the one we have to look at? → *5 is the digit in the tens column.*

4 What is that column worth? → *5 lots of 10 = 50*

5 Does your answer make sense? Yes? Then put in your answer. No? Then go back to Step 1.

H   T   U
359 = 300 + **50** + 9
Yes! My answer is correct!

Practice questions

Can you use the flow chart to help you answer these questions?

Write in the missing numbers.

	H	T	U			H	T	U
1 692 =	☐	+ 90 +	2		**5** 774 =	☐ +	☐	+ 4
2 743 = 700 +	☐	+ 3			**6** 326 = 300 +	☐	+ ☐	
3 551 = 500 +	50 +	☐			**7** 528 =	☐ +	☐	+ 8
4 896 =	☐	+ 90 +	6		**8** 999 =	☐ +	☐	+ ☐

Maths Star has a digit-mixing machine.

When he puts 3 digits in at the top, the machine mixes them up into the different numbers they can make.
Watch. Maths Star has put in 2, 5 and 7.

$$275 = 200 + 70 + 5$$

$$725 = 700 + 20 + 5$$

$$527 = 500 + 20 + 7$$

$$572 = 500 + 70 + 2$$

$$752 = 700 + 50 + 2$$

$$257 = 200 + 50 + 7$$

Practice questions

Can you find the six numbers that the mixing machine makes when Maths Star puts in the following digits?   8   6   3

1 _____ = ☐ + ☐ + ☐   **4** _____ = ☐ + ☐ + ☐

2 _____ = ☐ + ☐ + ☐   **5** _____ = ☐ + ☐ + ☐

3 _____ = ☐ + ☐ + ☐   **6** _____ = ☐ + ☐ + ☐

Put the numbers in order from smallest to largest.

smallest   largest

You could practise some more by putting 3 different numbers into the mixing machine!

Star Tip

Remember:
Single digit numbers are from 1 to 9
Two digit numbers are from 10 to 99
Three digit numbers are from 100 to 999

Star Tip

Always read numbers from left to right – just like words.

3 ➞ 5 ➞ 4

three hundred and fifty four

Reading measures

When you are reading measures, always check which units you are measuring.

Question: Harry is standing on the bathroom scales. How much does he weigh?

STAR STEPS

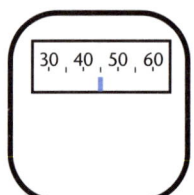

1 Read the question then read it again.

2 What am I measuring?   *How much Harry weighs.*

3 Which units am I using?   *Weight, the scales are labelled in kilograms.*

4 Read the scale.   *The arrow is pointing to 45 kg. Harry weighs 45 kg.*

5 Check your answer. Is it sensible?   *Yes, Harry would weigh 45 kg.*

Practice questions

1 **Harry takes his scales to school. All of his friends weigh themselves.**
Can you read how many kilograms they each weigh?

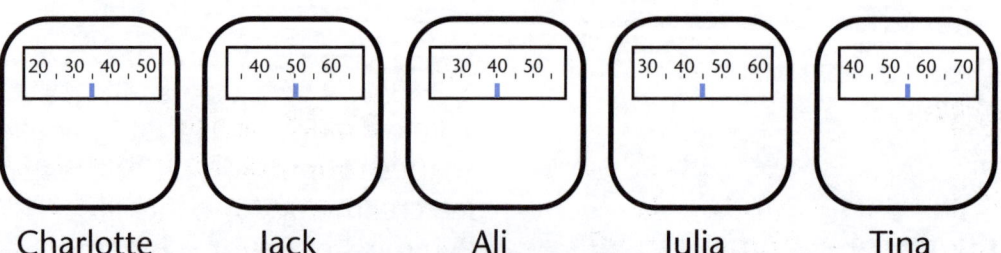

Charlotte   Jack   Ali   Julia   Tina

2 Harry decided to see how tall he is.
He measures himself on the class wall chart.
Harry's friends all do the same.

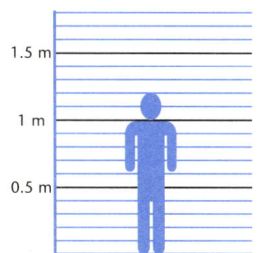

How tall are they?

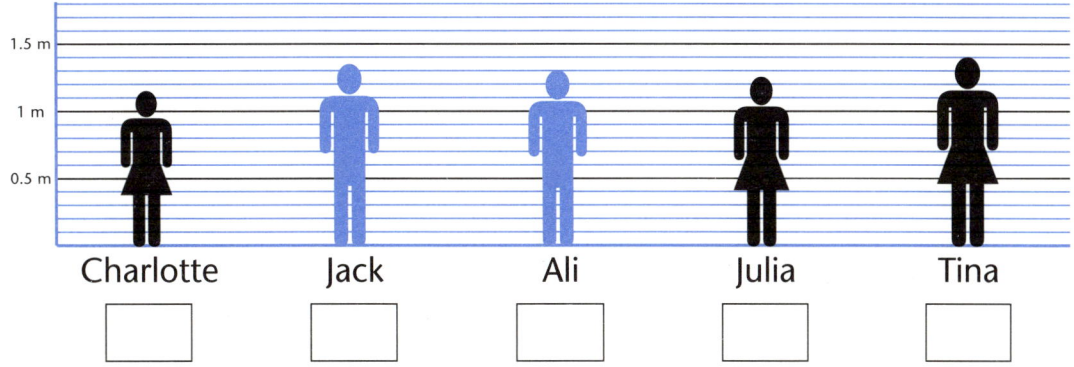

Charlotte	Jack	Ali	Julia	Tina

3 Harry wants to know how heavy and how tall his teacher is!
He asks Mrs West to stand on the scales.

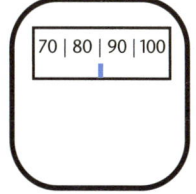

How much does Mrs West weigh? [ ]

4 Mrs West stands next to the wall chart.

How tall is Mrs West? [ ]

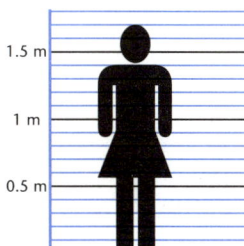

Challenge

How much taller and heavier is Mrs West than Harry and each of his friends?

Money

Money is all about place value too. Let's have a quick look at money. Look at the symbols and the decimal point.

£78.42	Tens	Units	Decimal Point	Tenths	Hundredths
	7	8	.	4	2

The decimal point separates the pounds (£) from the pence (p).

Question: **What is the total of these coins?**

 £2  £1  50p 20p

STAR STEPS

1 Read the question then read it again.

Total. I have to find out how much these add up to.

2 How should I set out my sum?

Add the coins together one at a time, starting with the largest.

£2 + £1 = £3

£3 + 50p = £3 and 50p

£3.50 + 20p = £3 and 70p.

3 Does your answer make sense? Yes? Then put in your answer. No? Then go back to Step 1.

Write your answer like this: £3.70

Practice questions

**Use the flow chart to help you answer these questions.
Find the totals of these coins.**

1 2p, 5p, 20p, £1

2 10p, £2, 50p

3 £2, £2, £1, 50p, 5p

4 20p, £2, 50p, 5p

5 1p, 2p, 5p, £1

Challenge question

What is the total of these coins?
1p, 2p, 5p, 10p, 20p,
50p, £1, £2

Practice questions

1 **Can you find the totals of these coins?**

a) £1   50p   1p   ☐

b) 50p   20p   10p   2p   ☐

c) £1   £1   £1   50p   5p   2p   1p   ☐

d) £1   50p   20p   10p   5p   2p   1p   ☐

2 **I have £2. Can you work out what change I would get if I bought these things?**

a) Toy doll – £1.50   ☐

b) Toy soldier – 90p   ☐

c) Sweets – 65p   ☐

d) Sweets – 65p and toy soldier – 90p   ☐

3 **Put these values in order from smallest to largest.**

£50.05, £5.50, £5.05, £50.50, £4.23, £42.30, £32.40, £3.24

smallest   largest

☐ ☐ ☐ ☐ ☐ ☐ ☐ ☐

Star Tip

Remember the decimal point separates the **£** from the **p**.

Star Tip

Always put in the symbol for **£** or **p** when answering questions about money.

Number bonds to 20

Maths Star is really good at doing adding
and subtracting in his head.
Can you do these in your head?

Here are some number bonds up to 20.
See how quickly you can do them!
Ask a friend to time you. See if you can beat your record.

11+ [ ] = 20   1 + [ ] = 20   21 – [ ] = 20

12+ [ ] = 20   2 + [ ] = 20   22 – [ ] = 20

13+ [ ] = 20   3 + [ ] = 20   23 – [ ] = 20

14+ [ ] = 20   4 + [ ] = 20   24 – [ ] = 20

15+ [ ] = 20   5 + [ ] = 20   25 – [ ] = 20

16+ [ ] = 20   6 + [ ] = 20   26 – [ ] = 20

17+ [ ] = 20   7 + [ ] = 20   27 – [ ] = 20

18+ [ ] = 20   8 + [ ] = 20   28 – [ ] = 20

19+ [ ] = 20   9 + [ ] = 20   29 – [ ] = 20

10 + [ ] = 20   30 – [ ] = 20

Time = [ ]   Record = [ ]

Practice questions

Now try these.

1 2 + 3 + 4 = [ ]   **4** 5 + 6 + 7 = [ ]

2 3 + 4 + 5 = [ ]   **5** 1 + 3 + 5 = [ ]

3 4 + 5 + 6 = [ ]   **6** 3 + 5 + 7 = [ ]

You can use your number bonds to work out larger sums in your head.

STAR STEPS

Question: **160 +** ☐ **= 200**

1 Read the question then read it again.

What number added to 160 makes 200?

2 Picture the numbers.

160
200

3 Remember your number bonds up to 20.

16 + 4 = 20

4 Does your answer make sense? If not, go back to Step 1.

160 + 40 = 200
Yes! I'm right. That makes it much easier to do.

Practice questions

Now try these questions.

1 70 + ☐ = 200

2 60 + ☐ = 200

3 170 + ☐ = 200

4 120 + ☐ = 200

5 260 − ☐ = 200

6 220 − ☐ = 200

7 290 − ☐ = 200

8 240 − ☐ = 200

Star Tip

Learning number bonds can be just as useful as learning your tables. Practice makes perfect.

Mental maths

Adding and subtracting numbers with two digits

Addition

How can you add two numbers in your head? How can you subtract two numbers without writing it down? There are lots of ways to do it and people use whichever way works best for them. I'll show you my way.

STAR STEPS Question: **What is 64 add 33?**

1 Read the question then read it again.

OK 64 + 33. I am being asked to ADD 33 onto 64.

2 Start at the number that's being added onto.

Start with the biggest number.

3 Now count on in your head the TENS of the number that you are adding.

T U
3 3

Now 64 + 3 tens:
*64, 74, 84, **94**!*

4 Now add on in your head the UNITS of the number that you are adding.

T U
3 3

94, 95, 96, 97!

5 Check your answer. Is it sensible? If not, go back to Step 1.

Yes. 64 + 33 = 97. I was right!

Practice questions

1	34 add 43	**6**	49 + 62
2	76 + 18	**7**	84 add 39
3	28 add 13	**8**	25 + 92
4	55 + 46	**9**	38 add 72
5	73 add 81	**10**	64 + 37

Star Tip

Playing games that need good mental maths skills is really useful. Darts is a good one.

Subtraction

You can do the same when you are subtracting two numbers by counting BACK instead of counting on.

STAR STEPS

Question: **What is 46 subtract 27?**

1 Read the question then read it again.

OK 46 subtract 27. I am being asked to count back 27 from 46.

2 Think about the question.

This is like 46 subtract 20 (2 tens) and then subtract 7 (7 units) from that answer!

3 Start with the TENS first.

46 subtract 20 is 26.

4 Now complete the UNITS.

26 subtract 7 is 19.

5 Check your answer. Is it sensible? If not, go back to Step 1.

Yes. 46 – 27 = 19. I was right!

Practice questions

1	81 subtract 44	**6**	63 – 44
2	72 take away 19	**7**	28 subtract 22
3	54 subtract 23	**8**	38 take away 25
4	96 minus 48	**9**	77 subtract 63
5	52 subtract 36	**10**	92 – 24

Star Tip

These ways of doing addition and subtraction are easier if you know the single digit sums by heart. (EXAMPLE: 5 – 3 = 2)

Addition of two and three digit numbers

Adding two digit numbers

There are a few different ways of adding numbers but the best is called partitioning.
Partitioning means to 'break the sum into easy steps'.
We're going to use a pencil and paper for this question. Let's give it a go!

STAR STEPS

Question: **63 + 35 =** ☐

1 Read the question then read it again.

2 Think about the tens and units.

$$T\ U\ +\ T\ U$$
$$6\ 3\ +\ 3\ 5\ =$$

3 Add the tens together.

$$T\ U\ +\ T\ U$$
$$6\ 3\ +\ 3\ 5\ =$$ $60 + 30 = 90$

4 Now add the units together.

$$T\ U\ +\ T\ U$$
$$6\ 3\ +\ 3\ 5\ =$$ $3 + 5 = 8$

5 Now add the two answers together.

$90 + 8 = 98$.
The answer is 98!

6 Check your answer. Is it sensible?

If so, put it in the box.
If not, go back to Step 1.

Adding three digit numbers

We can use the same method for adding three digit numbers.

$$H\ T\ U\ +\ H\ T\ U$$
$$2\ 4\ 6\ +\ 1\ 5\ 2\ =\ 398$$

$200 + 100 = 300$ $40 + 50 = 90$ $6 + 2 = 8$

$300 + 90 + 8 = 398$

Practice questions

1 $47 + 29 =$ ☐

2 $38 + 17 =$ ☐

3 $64 + 49 =$ ☐

4 $765 + 492 =$ ☐

5 $336 + 419 =$ ☐

6 $226 + 731 =$ ☐

Star Tip
Make sure you link the hundreds to hundreds, tens to tens and units to units.

Subtracting two digit numbers

You can use partitioning to subtract numbers – but the
Star Crew find it easier to use number lines and 'jump back'
to the answer!

We're going to use a pencil and paper for this question. Let's give it a go!

STAR STEPS

Question: **76 – 41 =** ⬚

1 Read the question then read it again.

2 Draw the sum on a number line.

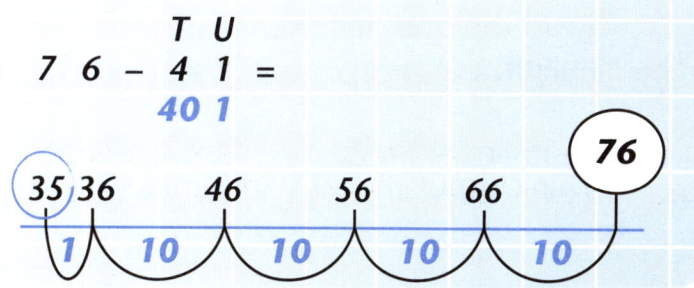

$$\begin{array}{c} T\ U \\ 7\ 6\ -\ 4\ 1\ = \\ 40\ 1 \end{array}$$

3 Check your answer. Is it sensible? If so, write it in the box

Yes. 76 – 41 = 35. I was right!

Subtracting three digit numbers

We can use the same approach for three digit numbers.

$$\begin{array}{c} H\ T\ U \\ 3\ 5\ 3\ -\ 1\ 3\ 4\ =\ 219 \\ 100\ 30\ 4 \end{array}$$

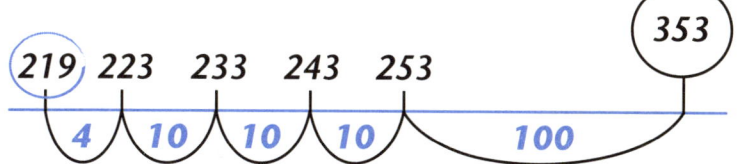

Addition

Number lines can also be used for addition.

$$\begin{array}{c} T\ U \\ 6\ 3\ +\ 3\ 5\ =\ 98 \\ 30\ 5 \end{array}$$

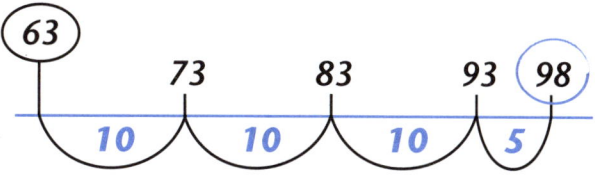

Practice questions

1 42 – 33 = ⬚   **4** 662 – 476 = ⬚

2 50 – 17 = ⬚   **5** 887 – 541 = ⬚

3 83 – 29 = ⬚   **6** 774 – 289 = ⬚

Star Tip

Remember, the digits have different values when they are in different columns.
219 = 200 + 10 + 9

Times tables and division facts

(2s, 3s, 4s, 5s and 10s!)

Learning your tables is like riding a bike.
Once you can do them you'll never forget them!

2x table test

You should know these, but go over them anyway.

1 x 2 = ☐

2 x 2 = ☐

☐ x 2 = 14

☐ x 2 = 6

4 x ☐ = 8

8 x 2 = ☐

☐ x 2 = 10

6 x 2 = ☐

☐ x 2 = 18

10 x ☐ = 20

3x table test

This one is a little harder – just try to remember them all!

1 x 3 = ☐

2 x 3 = ☐

3 x 3 = ☐

4 x 3 = ☐

5 x 3 = ☐

6 x 3 = ☐

7 x 3 = ☐

8 x 3 = ☐

9 x 3 = ☐

10 x 3 = ☐

4x table test

Four times tables are just double the answer to the 2 times tables.
Example: **5 x 2 = 10 so 5 x 4 = double 10 = 20!**

1 x 4 = ☐

2 x 4 = ☐

3 x 4 = ☐

4 x 4 = ☐

5 x 4 = ☐

6 x 4 = ☐

7 x 4 = ☐

8 x 4 = ☐

9 x 4 = ☐

10 x 4 = ☐

Star Tip

Learning tables makes the rest of your maths much easier.

5x table test

This is one of the easiest. Remember, the 5 times table answers ALWAYS end in 5 or 0.

1 x 5 = ☐   6 x 5 = ☐

2 x 5 = ☐   7 x 5 = ☐

3 x 5 = ☐   8 x 5 = ☐

4 x 5 = ☐   9 x 5 = ☐

5 x 5 = ☐   10 x 5 = ☐

10x table test

OK, this one is really easy. Each answer ends in a zero. You can just add a zero to the digit you are multiplying by!

1 x 10 = ☐   6 x 10 = ☐

2 x 10 = ☐   7 x 10 = ☐

3 x 10 = ☐   8 x 10 = ☐

4 x 10 = ☐   9 x 10 = ☐

5 x 10 = ☐   10 x 10 = ☐

Division

You should know that subtraction is the opposite of addition. Did you know that division is the opposite of multiplication? You do now!

Watch this:
8 x 2 = 16   and
(eight multiplied by two equals sixteen)

16 ÷ 2 = 8
(sixteen divided by two equals eight)
or
16 ÷ 8 = 2
(sixteen divided by eight equals two)

See if you can answer these sums. Use your tables to help you.

1   25 ÷ 5 = ☐

2   21 ÷ ☐ = 3

3   ☐ ÷ 10 = 4

4   24 ÷ ☐ = 3

5   36 ÷ ☐ = 4

6   ☐ ÷ 4 = 4

7   30 ÷ 10 = ☐

8   60 ÷ 5 = ☐

9   ☐ ÷ 3 = 3

10 18 ÷ ☐ = 9

11 ☐ ÷ 4 = 2

12 27 ÷ ☐ = 9

13 30 ÷ ☐ = 10

14 ☐ ÷ 10 = 8

15 45 ÷ ☐ = 5

Star Tip

See how quickly you can say the answers. Put them in a rhyme if that helps you!

Star Tip

Once you think you know a times table, ask a friend or relative to test you.

Number problems

Some maths questions have words as well as numbers. What you have to do is work out which words are important and which words aren't.

Question: **Finley needs 29 cartons of milkshake for his birthday party. There are 3 cartons in a pack.**

STAR STEPS

How many packs does he need to buy?

1 Read the question then read it again.

It's really important to read the question again because there are lots of words.

2 What is it asking you to do?

How many packs of milkshake does Finley need to buy?

3 Find the operation that you are going to use. Is it ADD, SUBTRACT, MULTIPLY or DIVIDE?

OK, he needs 29 cartons. There are 3 in a pack. How many 'lots' of 3 are there in 29? It's division.

4 Work out the sum including any remainders you may have. Draw a picture to help you.

29 ÷ 3 so | 3 | 6 | 9 | 12 | 15 | 18 | 21 | 24 | 27 |

27 is not enough as Finley needs 29 so I need one more. That makes 10 cartons.

$$\begin{array}{r} 9\ r\ 2 \\ 3\overline{)29} \\ \underline{27} \\ 2 \end{array}$$

5 Think about your final answer before putting it in the answer box.

Finley is going to need 10 packs because if he only bought 9 he would have 27 cartons (9 lots of 3)! Two people would be thirsty. If he buys 10 packs then everyone has a drink and there is one left over.

Star Tip

Never rush these questions. Always check your final answer. Does it make sense?

Try to answer these word problems using the method on page 28.

1 Leo puts 14 stickers into his album. Each page holds 5 stickers.
How many pages does he need?

☐ pages

2 Mrs Dough buys 7 packets of chocolate cookies. There are 8 cookies
in each packet. How many cookies does she have altogether?

☐ cookies

3 James had 48 marbles in a bag but dropped them all on the floor!
When he picked them up he could only find 37. How many marbles
has he lost?

☐ marbles

4 Chandeep has 3 cats, 2 dogs and a budgie. How many legs do her
pets have altogether?

☐ legs

5 Lisa gives her 24 classmates a card each at Christmas. There are 5
cards in a box. How many boxes does she need?

☐ boxes

Star Tip
Remember to work out WHAT you need to do first (add, subtract, multiply or
divide). Think of the different words that might give you a clue.

Fractions

Let's start with the basics of fractions.
A fraction is 'part of a whole number'.

$\dfrac{1}{2}$

the numerator — The numerator tells you how many equal parts there are.

$\dfrac{1}{2}$ is 1 part of 2

the – means 'part of'

the denominator — The denominator tells you the number of equal parts the whole number is divided into.

Fractions that have the same value are called **equivalent** fractions.

$\dfrac{1}{2}$ 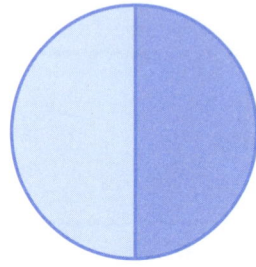 is the same as $\dfrac{2}{4}$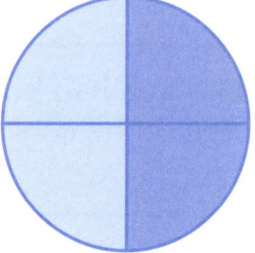

$\dfrac{1}{4}$ 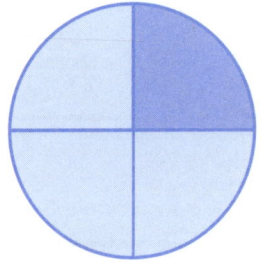 is the same as $\dfrac{2}{8}$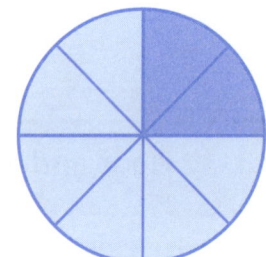

To achieve Level 3 you need to be able to recognise fractions that are the same or equivalent.
Try to learn these ones off by heart.

$$\dfrac{1}{2} = \dfrac{2}{4} = \dfrac{3}{6} = \dfrac{4}{8} = \dfrac{5}{10}$$

$$\dfrac{1}{4} = \dfrac{2}{8} = \dfrac{3}{12} = \dfrac{4}{16} = \dfrac{5}{20}$$

Practice questions

1 **Colour fractions of these shapes.**

a) $\frac{3}{8}$

d) $\frac{1}{2}$

b) $\frac{5}{12}$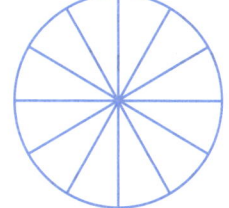

e) $\frac{7}{8}$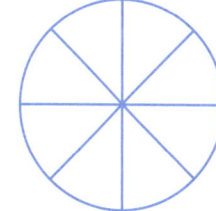

c) $\frac{1}{2}$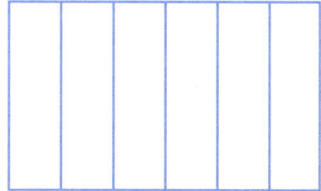

f) $\frac{7}{12}$

2 **Now try these sweets problems.**

a) $\frac{1}{2}$ of 16 sweets is ☐ sweets.

b) $\frac{1}{2}$ of 6 sweets is ☐ sweets.

c) $\frac{3}{8}$ of 16 sweets is ☐ sweets.

d) $\frac{1}{2}$ of 8 sweets is ☐ sweets.

Star Tip

Remember, the number on the bottom of the fraction (denominator) is the number of equal parts the whole number is divided into.
The number on the top of the fraction (numerator) is the number of those parts in that fraction.

2D and 3D shapes

2D shapes

★ 2D shapes are 'flat shapes'.
★ If they have straight sides they are called 'polygons'.
★ If they have straight sides and all their angles are equal, they are called 'regular polygons'.

Here are some 2D shapes you should know:

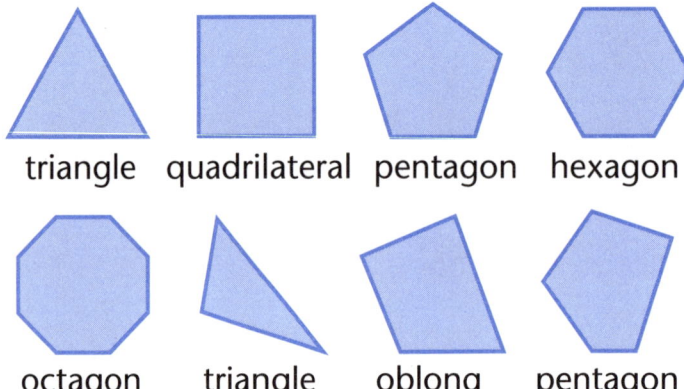

triangle   quadrilateral   pentagon   hexagon

octagon   triangle   oblong   pentagon

Symmetry

A shape is symmetrical if both sides are the same when a mirror line is drawn. This is also called 'reflective symmetry'.

Look:

1 line of symmetry

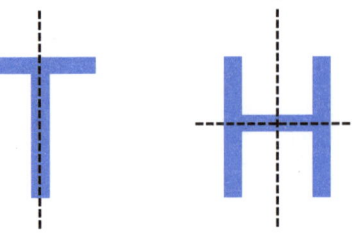

2 lines of symmetry

Can you draw the reflection of each of these shapes?
Now can you name each of these polygons?

Star Tip

Try to use things you know to remember how many sides polygons have.
Examples:
TRIcycle (3 wheels) = TRIangle (3 sides)
QUADbike (4 wheels) = QUADrilateral (4 sides)
OCTopus (8 legs) = OCTagon (8 sides)

3D shapes

3D shapes can also be
called solid shapes.
Take a look at this cube.

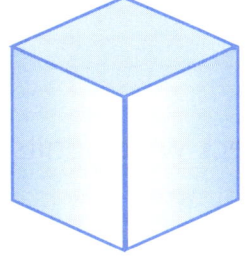

It has 8 corners or vertices.
It has 12 edges.
It has 6 faces (like a dice).
Go on, count them!

Here are some 3D shapes you should know:

Cone

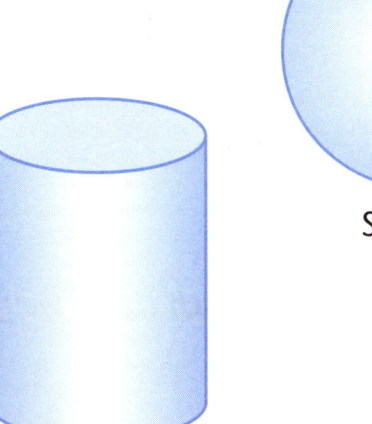

Cylinder

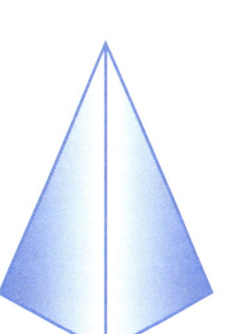

Sphere

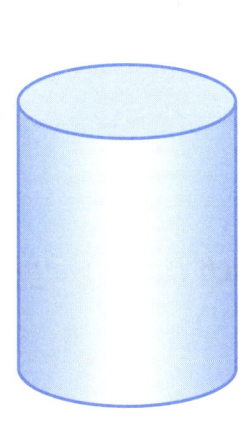

Pyramid

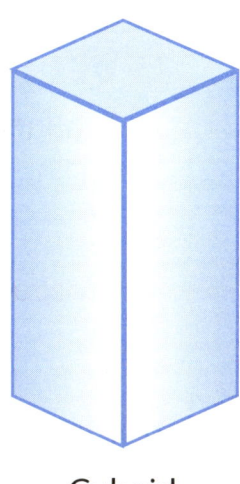

Cuboid

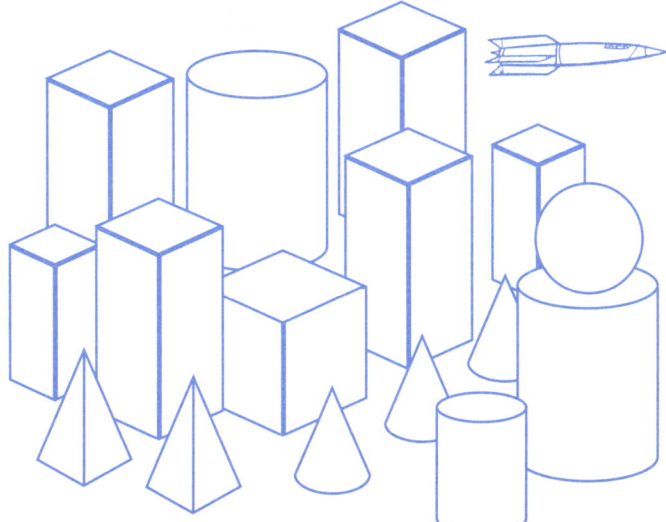

Can you colour in this picture of
'Star City' using the following key?

Cone = blue
Cylinder = red
Cuboid = purple
Cube = brown
Pyramid = green
Sphere = Yellow

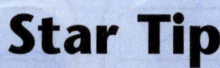

Star Tip

Think about things that look like 3D
shapes to remind you of their names.
Ice cream cone = cone
Pyramids of Egypt = pyramid
Football = sphere

Measures

It is important to learn how to read scales and measure accurately for distance, time, weight and capacity. Try some of these measures.

Distance

1 Measure these lines.

a) ━━━━━━━━━━━━━━━━━ ☐ cm

b) ━━━━━━━━━━━━━━━━━━━━━ ☐ cm

c) ━━━━━━━━ ☐ cm

Weight

2 What weight is shown on each of these scales?

a) ☐ g

b) ☐ g

c) ☐ g

Capacity

3 How much liquid is in these jugs?

a) ☐ ml

b) ☐ ml

c) ☐ ml

Time

4 Try these questions:

a) How many minutes to 6:00 o'clock? ☐

b) How many days until Christmas? ☐

Dec **19**

c) How many minutes to midnight? ☐

Star Tip

Don't forget to learn the abbreviations for all the different units.
Examples: **kg = kilograms, ml = millilitres, m = metres**

Use the measurement facts on the previous page to try to answer these questions.

Distance

1 How many centimetres are there in:

2 metres? ☐

6 metres? ☐

8 metres? ☐

2 If your pencil case is 15 cm long, how many 3 cm rulers could you fit inside end to end? ☐ rulers

Weight

3 If a man weighs 70 kg and a child weighs half the man's weight, how much does the child weigh?

☐ kg

4 One aeroplane weighs 20 tons. What do 7 aeroplanes weigh? ☐ tons

5 Which weighs more: a kg of stones or a kilogram of leaves?

☐

Capacity

6 My bath is filled with 45 litres of water. 22 litres goes down the plug hole. How much is left? ☐ l

7 I drink 4 cups of tea each day. Each cup holds 250 ml of tea. How many litres of tea do I drink each day?

☐ l

8 How many millilitres are there in 2 litres of orange juice? ☐ ml

Time

9 How many days are there in 3 weeks? ☐ days

10 How many weeks is it until your birthday? ☐ weeks

11 How many minutes are there in $\frac{1}{2}$ an hour? ☐ minutes

Star Tip

Remember to read the question then read it again to make sure you understand what each question is asking you.

Looking at tables and lists

Information can be shown to you in many ways.
This is some information about the Star Crew!

Likes or enjoys	Maths Star	Reading Star	Writing Star
Going to school	✔	✔	✔
Playing sports	✘	✔	✔
Playing a musical instrument	✔	✘	✘
Drawing and painting	✘	✔	✔
Reading comics	✔	✔	✘
Eating cakes and sweets	✔	✔	✔
Riding a bike	✔	✘	✔
Computer games	✔	✘	✘
Cooking	✘	✔	✘

Read the table. What does it tell you?

Now I'm going to give you a quiz to see how much you know about the Star Crew. When you have finished, check your score on the table below to see how well you did.

Ready… here we go!

1 Which star doesn't like riding a bike?

2 Which star can play a musical instrument?

3 How many stars don't like cooking?

4 Which stars enjoy playing sports?

5 How many stars don't like cakes and sweets?

6 Which stars like going to school?

7 Which star doesn't like reading comics?

8 How many things does Maths Star enjoy?

9 How many things does Writing Star enjoy?

10 Which two things do all the stars enjoy?

How did you do?

My score:

Your score	Star score
1 to 3	Twinkle Star
4 to 7	Rising Star
8 to 9	Shining Star
10	Super Star

Bar graphs and charts

Graphs and charts show information in an easy-to-read way.
These are the steps for working with graphs and charts:

1 Read each question then read it again.
2 Look to see what each axis is showing.
3 Read the information you find carefully.
4 Check each answer.

Bar graph

This is a bar graph to show the number of vehicles Class 3A
saw in a traffic survey.

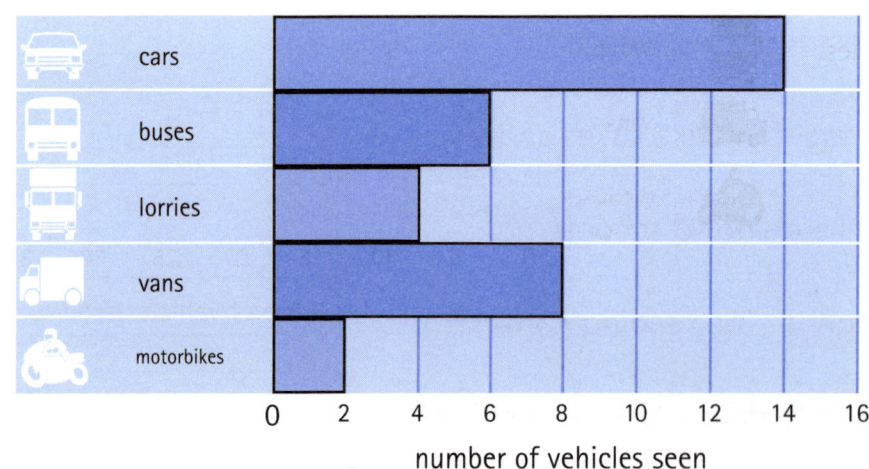

Look at the bar graph above and answer these questions.

1 How many buses were seen?

2 How many vans were seen?

3 How many more cars were there than lorries?

4 What was the total number of motorbikes and buses?

5 How many fewer buses were there than vans?

6 Which type of vehicle was seen 4 times?

Tally chart

Class 3B also did a traffic survey the following week. They recorded their results on a tally chart.

vehicle		tally	total
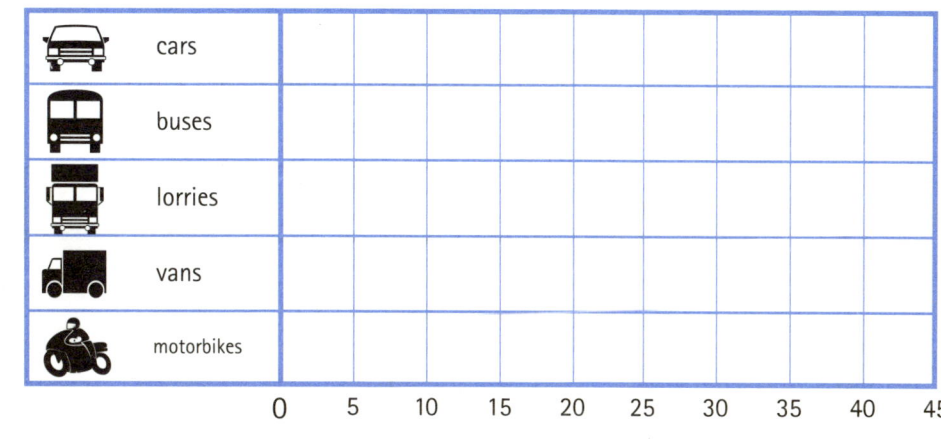 cars		HHT HHT HHT HHT HHT HHT HHT HHT	
buses		HHT HHT HHT	
lorries		HHT HHT HHT HHT HHT	
vans		HHT HHT HHT HHT HHT HHT HHT	
motorbikes		HHT	

Can you add up the total for each vehicle and put the results onto this bar chart?

vehicles — cars, buses, lorries, vans, motorbikes

0 5 10 15 20 25 30 35 40 45

number of vehicles seen

Pictogram

A pictogram uses symbols to show a group of units.

Can you draw a pictogram for Class 3A's data?
The first one has been done for you.

Key

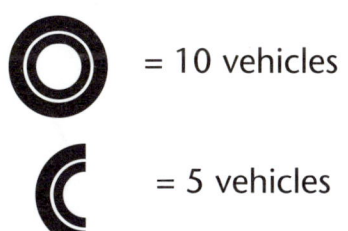 = 10 vehicles

= 5 vehicles

Cars	◎ ◎ ◎ ◎
Buses	
Lorries	
Vans	
Motorbikes	

Star Tip

Use a ruler when you are drawing graphs – you must be accurate.

KEY FACTS

Place value

Each number is made up from digits. Where these digits are in a number gives that number its value.

	Hundreds	Tens	Units	
784	7	8	4	= 700 + 80 + 4

Single digit numbers are from 1 to 9
Two digit numbers are from 10 to 99
Three digit numbers are from 100 to 999

Negative numbers

Negative numbers are just numbers LESS than 0.

We write them like this: −1   −2   −3   −4
and we say: "minus 1"   "minus 2"   "minus 3"   "minus 4"

Times tables

2 times table – double the number you are multiplying (always end in an even number)
3 times table – there's no easy way to remember these. You just have to learn them by heart.
4 times table – answers are always twice the two times table ones!
5 times table – answers always end in a 5 or a 0.
10 times table – answers always end in 0. Put a 0 after the number you are multiplying.

Word problems

Always read the question twice and circle the words that are telling you WHAT to do.

Fractions

A fraction is 'part of a whole number'.

$\dfrac{1}{2}$

1 the numerator   The numerator tells you how many equal parts there are.

2 the denominator   The denominator tells you the number of equal parts the whole number is divided into.

Fractions that have the same value are called **equivalent** fractions:

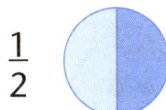 $\frac{1}{2}$ is the same as $\frac{2}{4}$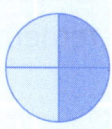

 $\frac{1}{3}$ is the same as $\frac{2}{6}$

2D and 3D shapes

2D shapes are 'flat shapes'.
If they have straight sides they are called 'polygons'.
If they have straight sides and all their angles are equal, they are called 'regular polygons'.

A shape is symmetrical if both sides are the same when a mirror line is drawn. This is also called 'reflective symmetry'.

Here are some names of 3D shapes.

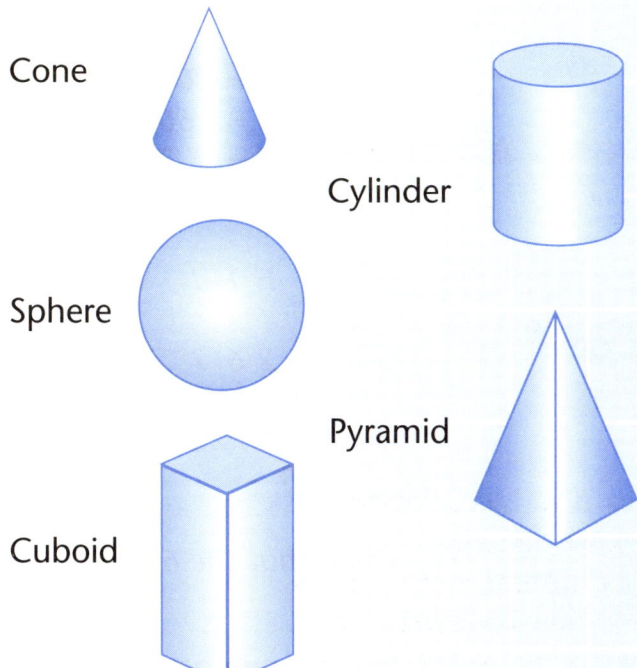

Cone

Cylinder

Sphere

Pyramid

Cuboid

Measures
Distance – length – how long, tall or far
10 millimetres = 1 centimetre
(10 mm = 1 cm)
100 centimetres = 1 metre
(100 cm = 1 m)

1000 metres = 1 kilometre
(1000 m = 1 km)

Weight – how heavy (or light)
1000 grams = 1 kilogram (1000 g = 1 kg)
1000 kilograms = 1 ton
(1000 kg = 1 ton)

Capacity – how much in a bowl or jug (mainly liquids)
1000 millilitres = 1 litre (1000 ml = 1 l)

Time – how old, how soon
60 seconds = 1 minute
60 minutes = 1 hour
24 hours = 1 day
7 days = 1 week
365 days = 1 year (except a leap year which has 366 days – 2004 is a leap year)
52 weeks = 1 year
100 years = 1 century
1000 years = 1 millennium

Handling data

Graphs and charts show information in an easy-to-read way.
These are the steps for working with graphs and charts:

1 Read each question then read it again.
2 Look to see what each axis is showing.
3 Read the information you find carefully.
4 Check each answer.

The Key Stage 1 Tests

What are SATs?

The Key Stage 1 National Tests, or SATs as they are commonly known, are assessments that take place at the end of Year 2. There are tests in Reading, Writing and Maths and these are supported by Teacher Assessment in all three areas.

The tests are usually carried out during May and are spread out over several weeks to ease the pressure on the children. They take place as part of a normal day and most schools do not tell the children they are doing a 'test'. The children will have done plenty of practices and preparation in school and the tests are usually carried out in the classroom with the teacher.

What do the levels mean?

The National Curriculum sets down levels children are expected to reach by certain ages. On average children will be at

- **Level 2 by the end of Key Stage 1 (age 7)**
- **Level 4 by the end of Key Stage 2 (age 11)**
- **Level 5/6 at the end of Key Stage 3 (age 14)**

Within each level there are strands A, B and C where A indicates the child is working confidently within the level, B is average and C shows they are just achieving within the level.

What do the tests consist of?

Writing

There are two Writing Tasks, a Spelling Test and a Handwriting Task.
The Writing Tasks consist of a longer task, which is usually in the form of a story, and a shorter task, which will take a different form, perhaps a letter or a set of instructions. The children will be expected to work independently and spell and punctuate their work as best they can. The tasks are not timed but it is expected that the longer task should take about 45 minutes and the shorter one about 30 minutes.

There is also a separate Spelling Test where children are required to write a list of words read out by the teacher. There are about 20 words and the majority of them will be words the children have already come across.

Handwriting is also looked at. In some cases handwriting is assessed as part of the Writing Tasks. Children might be asked to copy out a part of their story in their best handwriting and will be expected to join some letters.

Reading

The Reading Test consists of a reading task and a separate comprehension test. During the reading task the child will read part of a book to a teacher and should be able to discuss the book and answer questions. Their ability to work out unknown words, read with good pace and expression and show an understanding of the story are all assessed.

For the reading comprehension test the children are given a reading booklet with a story and piece of non-fiction writing in. The children will be expected to read as much as they can independently and answer the questions that are in the booklet.

Maths

All children will take a written Maths Test. It covers most aspects of Number and Shape, Space and Measuring. There are also some mental maths questions that the teacher will read out. There is an emphasis on Using and Applying mathematical knowledge and children are often asked to solve simple problems and explain their answers.

What is the Teacher Assessment?

At the end of Key Stage 1 teachers also carry out their own assessments of each child in the areas of Reading, Writing and Maths. These assessments are based on classroom observations and looking at a child's work over a period of time. Usually the Teacher Assessment level is the same as the SATs level but occasionally there are discrepancies. It is worth remembering that the SATs level is an indication of how your child performed on one particular day under test-like conditions and only covers small areas of the curriculum. The Teacher Assessment gives a more rounded view of the child's ability and covers all aspects of the English and Maths curriculums.

Helping your child do well

There is no right way to prepare your child and it is not necessary to spend hours revising for a test. Most children do not even know they are doing a test and this is the best preparation for them!

Most schools do not tell the children they are taking a test as this adds a huge amount of pressure on them to get it all right. They will have had opportunities to try practice papers, doing as much as they can independently. When the real test comes it is usually seen as just another classroom activity.

Working at home with your child

Working through these books with your child will help reinforce what they have learnt during Year 2 and get them used to answering test type questions. Here are some things you can do:

- Find time when you are both relaxed and happy.
- Choose a quiet spot without distractions.
- Keep sessions short, especially when you see your child is getting bored or frustrated.
- Work through examples in this book together and then allow your child to have a go at the practice questions. Read the *Star Tips* together – you could ask your child to come up with different voices for the characters!
- Encourage them if they find something difficult. Try not to let your frustrations show, as they will pick up on this and become more anxious themselves. Take a short break and try again tomorrow.
- Try to make all activities meaningful for them. When practising writing letters, why not write one to a friend or relative? This will encourage them to practise their reading when they get a reply! Or ask them to write out your shopping list for you. Let them play with your money and encourage them to work out totals and calculate change using real coins.

All children will find questions on the papers that they cannot do or find very challenging and some can find this hard to cope with. You can help by encouraging them to have a go at something difficult and not to give up when it gets tough. A challenging jigsaw puzzle is a good place to start.

Of course, preparation does not always have to take the form of pencil and paper work. Children learn by doing so try some fun practical activities:

- **Read to your child. This will help greatly with their writing as they learn about story structure and acquire new vocabulary.**
- **Ask your child to tell you a bedtime story for a change.**
- **Play games. Board games such as snakes and ladders or dominoes are great for all those number skills. Use long car journeys for word games.**
- **Play shops with REAL money!**

Often children's concerns or worries about the tests come from parents' own concerns about their child. Unless your child's school tells the children they are doing a test, try not to talk to them, or in front of them, about the tests. Keep things as normal as possible during the test period and take opportunities to celebrate their success. A word of praise from a parent goes a long way!

Good luck and have fun!

Answers

Page 6
Section 1
1) 5
2) 4
3) 3
4) 2
5) 1
6) 0
7) 5
8) 4
9) 3
10) 2
11) 1
12) 0

Section 2
1) 5
2) 4
3) 3
4) 2
5) 1
6) 0
7) 5
8) 5
9) 5
10) 5
11) 5
12) 5

Page 7
Section 1
1) 10
2) 9
3) 8
4) 7
5) 6
6) 5
7) 4
8) 3
9) 2
10) 1
11) 0
12) 10
13) 9
14) 8
15) 7
16) 6
17) 5
18) 4
19) 3
20) 2
21) 1
22) 0

Section 2
1) 10
2) 11
3) 12
4) 13
5) 14
6) 15
7) 16
8) 17
9) 18
10) 19
11) 20
12) 1
13) 5
14) 3
15) 1
16) 4
17) 0
18) 1
19) 5
20) 3
21) 5
22) 8

Page 9
Left hand column
321
759
273
914
475
132
647
519
Right hand column
9
30
400
20
500
70
50
600

Page 10
1) 5
2) 26
3) 51
4) 15
5) 61
6) 25

Page 11
Trevor has 21 sweets

Page 12
The big doll is 9 blocks taller than the short doll.
Answers will vary in the explanation but children should circle the word "taller".

Page 14
1) 600
2) 40
3) 1
4) 800
5) 700 and 70
6) 20 and 6
7) 500 and 20
8) 900 and 90 and 9

Page 15
800 + 60 + 3 = 863
800 + 30 + 6 = 836
600 + 80 + 3 = 683
600 + 30 + 8 = 638
300 + 60 + 8 = 368
300 + 80 + 6 = 386

Largest number is 863 and the smallest is 368

Page 16 – 17
1) Scales from Left to Right: 35 kg, 50 kg, 40 kg, 45 kg, 55 kg
2) Harry is 120 cm. Others from left to right: 115 cm, 135 cm, 130 cm, 125 cm, 140 cm.
3) 85 kg
4) 170 cm

Challenge
Mrs West is 40 kg heavier and 50 cm taller than Harry.
Mrs West is 50 kg heavier and 55 cm taller than Charlotte.
Mrs West is 35 kg heavier and 35 cm taller than Jack.
Mrs West is 45 kg heavier and 40 cm taller than Ali.
Mrs West is 40 kg heavier and 45 cm taller than Julia.
Mrs West is 30 kg heavier and 30 cm taller than Tina.

Page 18
1) £1.27
2) £2.60
3) £5.55
4) £2.75
5) £1.08
Challenge £3.88

Page 19
1 a) £1.51
  b) 82p
  c) £3.58
  d) £1.88
2 a) 50p
  b) £1.10
  c) £1.35
  d) 45p
3) Smallest to largest: £3.24, £4.23, £5.05, £5.50, £32.40, £42.30, £50.05, £50.50

Page 20
First Column
9, 8, 7, 6, 5, 4, 3, 2, 1
Second Column
19, 18, 17, 16, 15, 14, 13, 12, 11, 10
Third Column
1, 2, 3, 4, 5, 6, 7, 8, 9, 10
Practice Questions
1) 9
2) 12
3) 15
4) 18
5) 9
6) 15

Page 21
1) 130
2) 140
3) 30
4) 80
5) 60
6) 20
7) 90
8) 40

Page 22
1) 77
2) 94
3) 41
4) 101
5) 154
6) 111
7) 123
8) 117
9) 110
10) 101

Page 23
1) 37
2) 53
3) 31
4) 48
5) 16
6) 19
7) 6
8) 13
9) 14
10) 68

Page 24
1) 76
2) 55
3) 113
4) 1257
5) 755
6) 957

Page 25
1) 9
2) 33
3) 54
4) 206
5) 346
6) 485

Page 26
2x table test
1 x 2 = 2
2 x 2 = 4
3 x 2 = 6
4 x 2 = 8
5 x 2 = 10
6 x 2 = 12
7 x 2 = 14
8 x 2 = 16
9 x 2 = 18
10 x 2 = 20
3x table test
1 x 3 = 3
2 x 3 = 6
3 x 3 = 9
4 x 3 = 12
5 x 3 = 15
6 x 3 = 18
7 x 3 = 21
8 x 3 = 24
9 x 3 = 27
10 x 3 = 30
4x table test
1 x 4 = 4
2 x 4 = 8
3 x 4 = 12
4 x 4 = 16
5 x 4 = 20
6 x 4 = 24
7 x 4 = 28
8 x 4 = 32
9 x 4 = 36
10 x 4 = 40

Page 27

5x table test

1 x 5 = 5
2 x 5 = 10
3 x 5 = 15
4 x 5 = 20
5 x 5 = 25
6 x 5 = 30
7 x 5 = 35
8 x 5 = 40
9 x 5 = 45
10 x 5 = 50

10x table test

1 x 10 = 10
2 x 10 = 20
3 x 10 = 30
4 x 10 = 40
5 x 10 = 50
6 x 10 = 60
7 x 10 = 70
8 x 10 = 80
9 x 10 = 90
10 x 10 = 100

Division

1) 5
2) 7
3) 40
4) 8
5) 9
6) 16
7) 3
8) 12
9) 9
10) 2
11) 8
12) 3
13) 3
14) 80
15) 9

Page 29

1) 3
2) 56
3) 11
4) 22
5) 5

Page 31

1) a)   d)

   b)   e)

   c)   f)

2) a) 8 sweets
   b) 3 sweets
   c) 6 sweets
   d) 4 sweets

Page 32

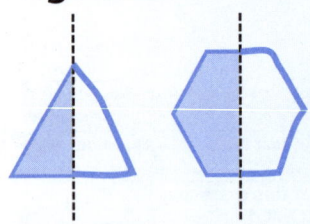

Page 33

Check to see that the correct shapes have been coloured the correct colours.

Page 34

1) a) 5.5 cm
   b) 7.5 cm
   c) 3 cm
2) a) 350 g
   b) 625 g
   c) 150 g
3) a) 500 ml
   b) 300 ml
   c) 750 ml
4) a) 15 minutes
   b) 6 days
   c) 90 minutes

Page 35

1) 200 cm, 600 cm, 800 cm
2) 5 rulers
3) 35 kg
4) 140 tons
5) They weigh the same.
6) 23 litres
7) 1 litre
8) 2000 ml
9) 21 days
10) Answers will vary.
11) 30 minutes

Page 37

1) Reading Star
2) Maths Star
3) Two
4) Reading and Writing Star
5) None
6) All of them
7) Writing Star
8) 6 things
9) 5 things
10) Going to school and eating cakes and sweets

Page 38

1) 6 buses
2) 8 vans
3) 10 more cars than lorries
4) 8 motorbikes and buses
5) 2 fewer buses than vans
6) Lorries were seen 4 times

Page 39

Totals in tally chart
Cars – 40
Buses – 15
Lorries – 25
Vans – 35
Motorbikes – 5

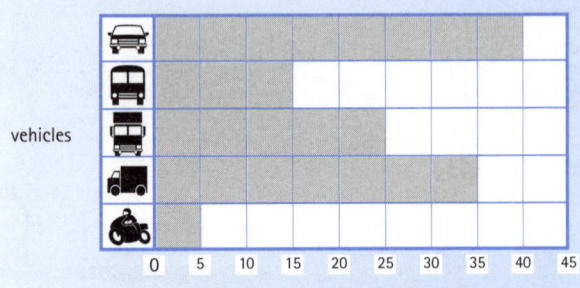